www.FlowerpotPress.com
PAB-0808-0191 · 978-1-4867-1580-0
Made in China/Fabriqué en Chine

FINN'S FUN TRUCKS
FRIENDLY FLIERS

Written by Finn Coyle Illustrated by Srimalie Bassani

We are the friendly fliers.
We fly some really awesome machines.

Each one has a job of its own.
Can you guess what each one does?

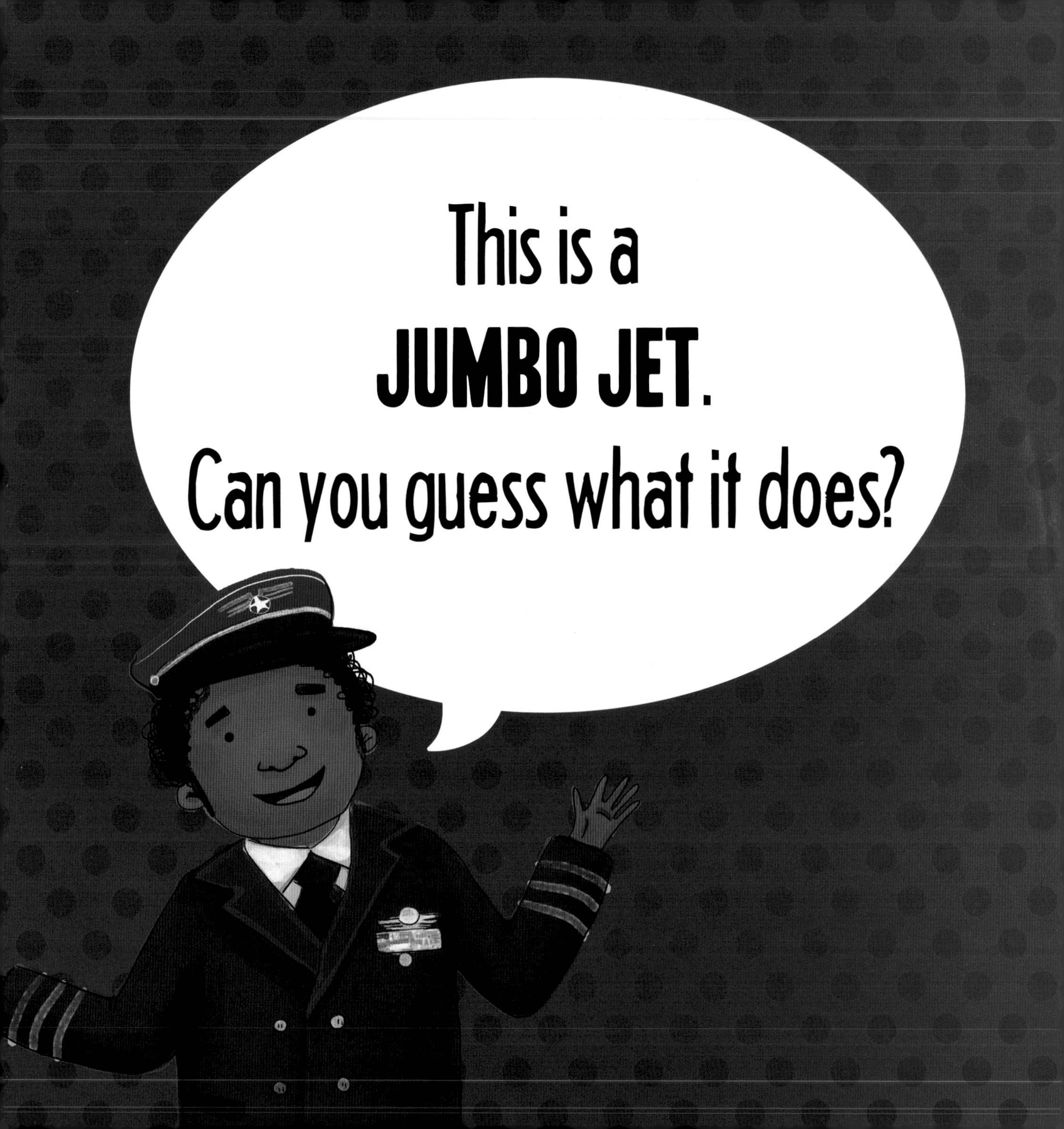
This is a
JUMBO JET.
Can you guess what it does?

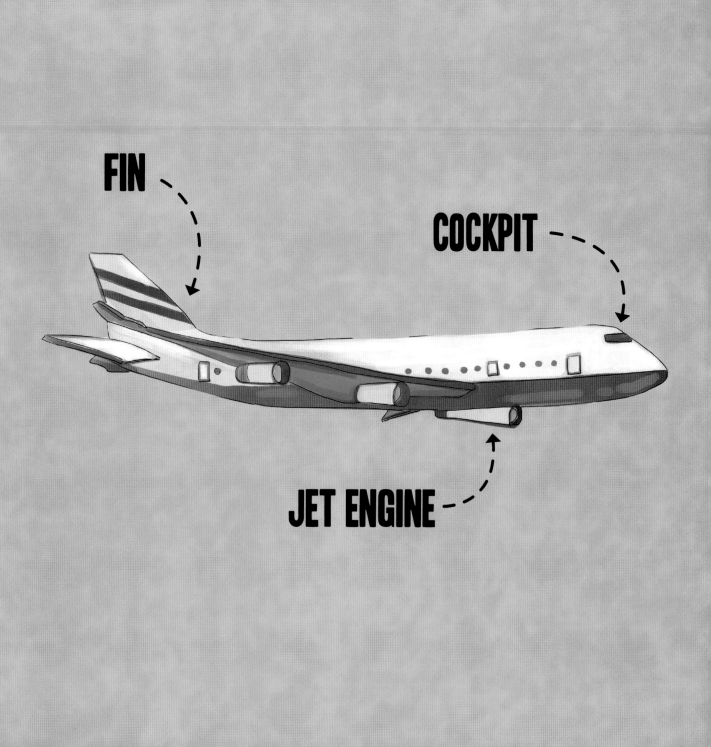

FIN

COCKPIT

JET ENGINE

A jumbo jet is used to carry people from place to place.

It takes off and lands at big airports because it needs a long runway to get going and to slow down.

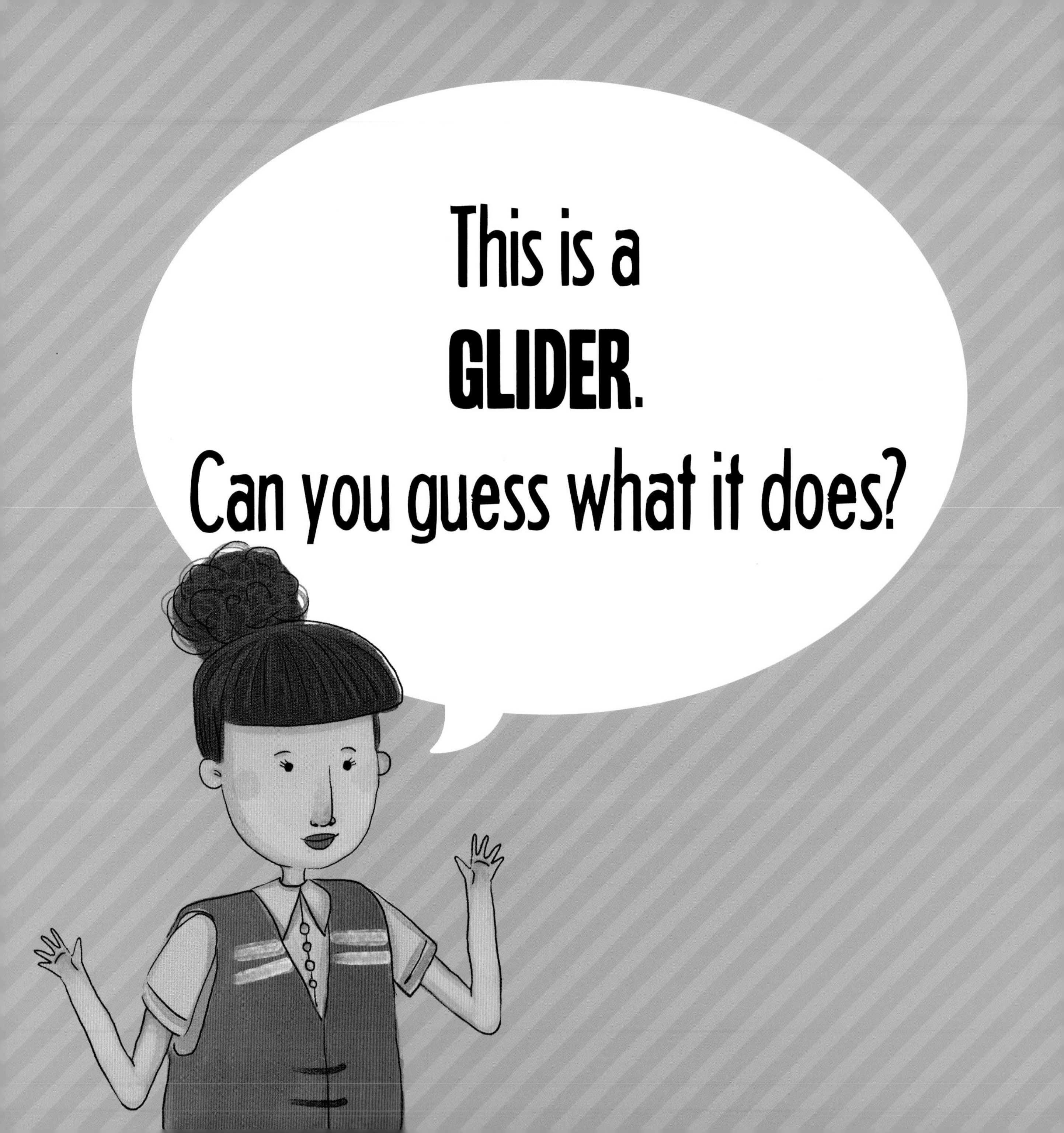
This is a
GLIDER.
Can you guess what it does?

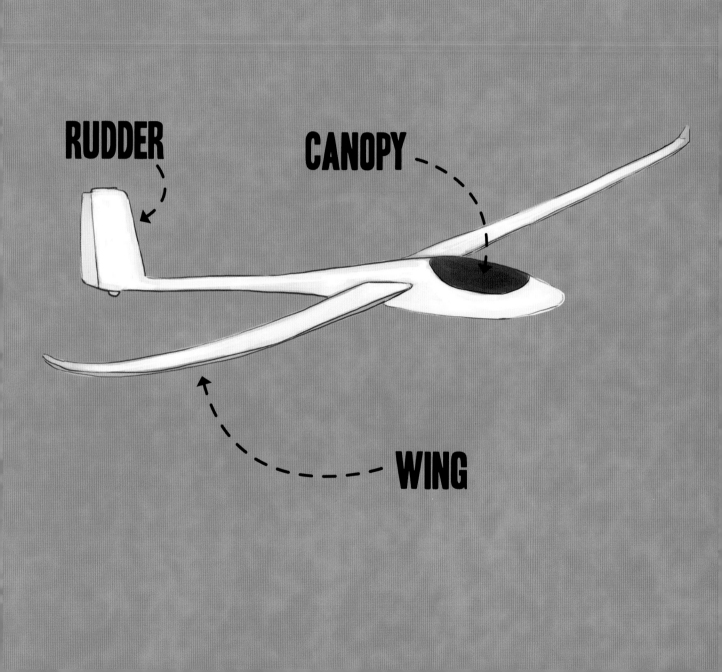

A glider is used for flying very quietly through the sky using no engine at all.

It gets pulled up into the sky by another plane and then uses its big wings to take a long, slow glide back to Earth.

This is a **SEAPLANE**.

Can you guess what it does?

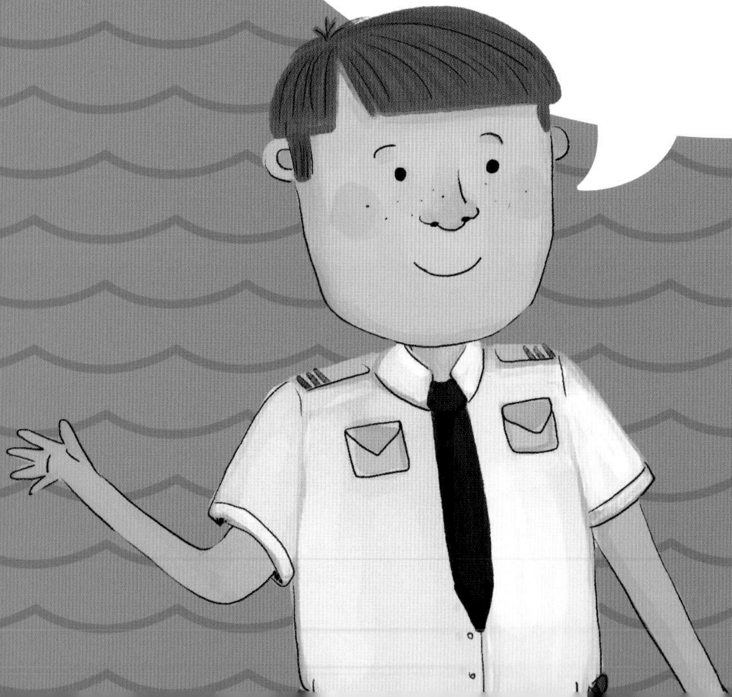

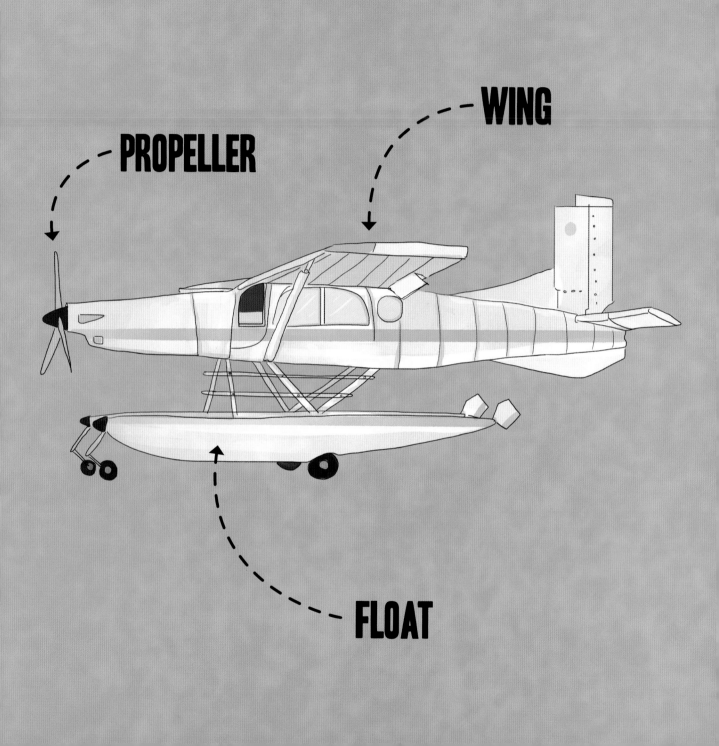

A seaplane is used in special locations where the pilot wants to take off or land on water.

Because of its specially designed bottom,
a seaplane can land on either water or land.

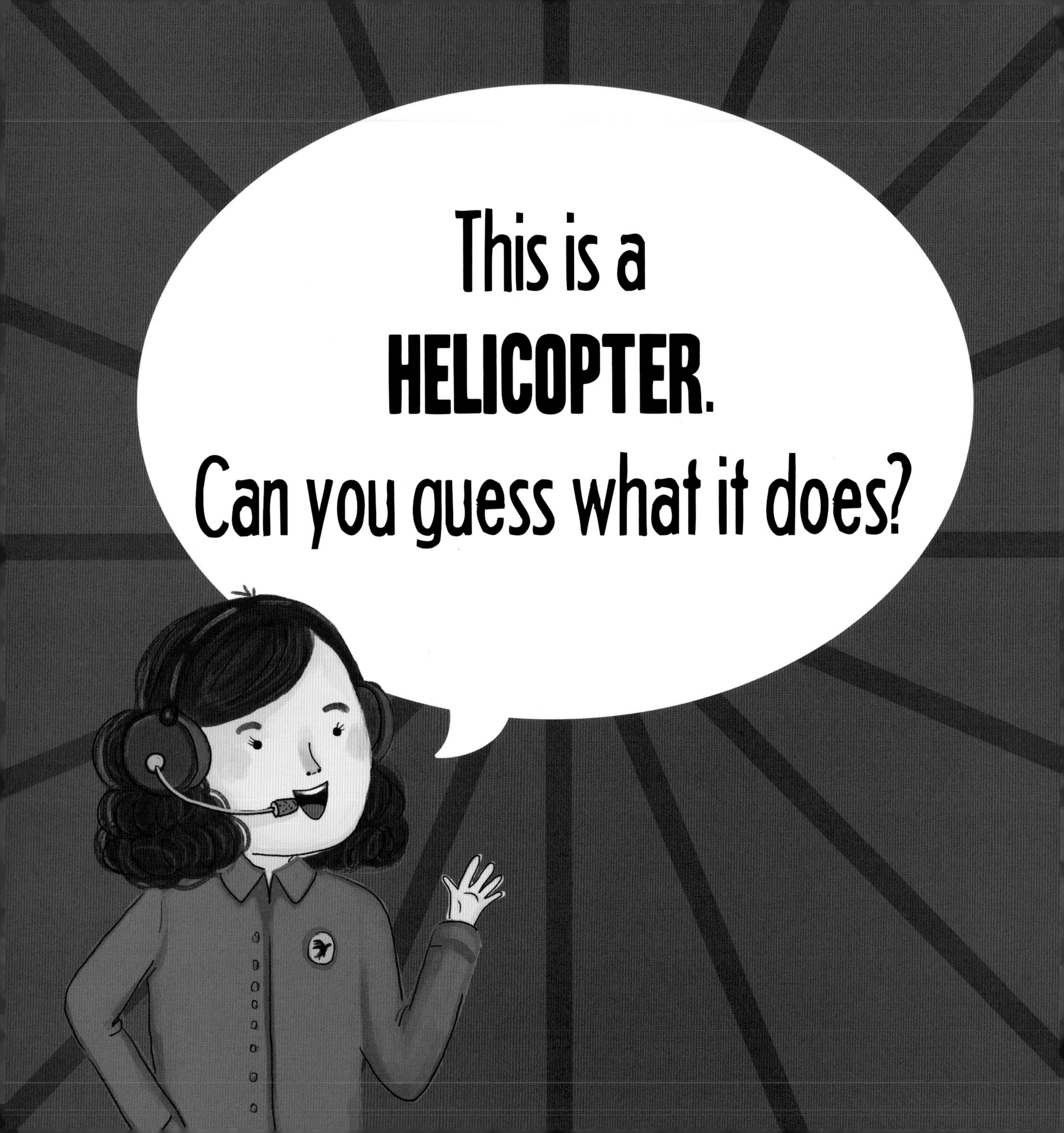
This is a
HELICOPTER.
Can you guess what it does?

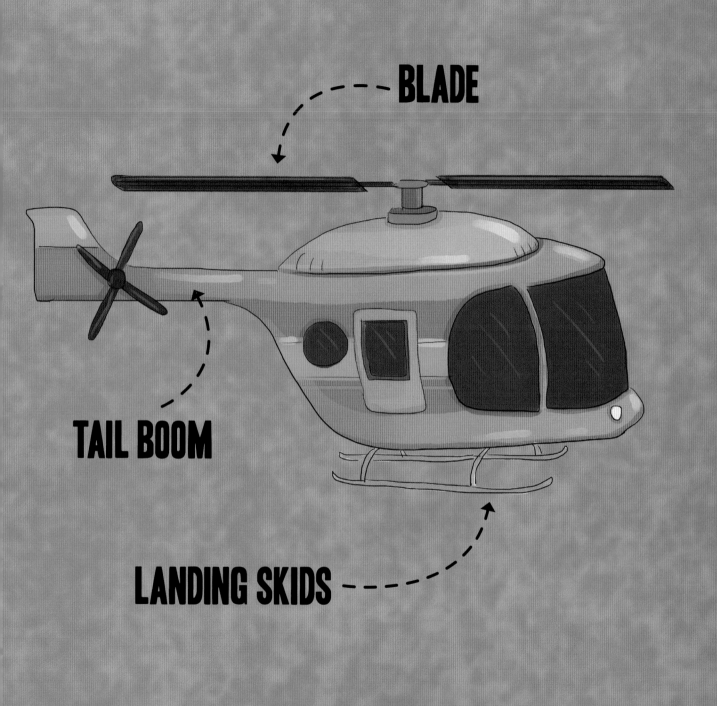

A helicopter can fly straight up and down.

This makes flying possible when there isn't enough room for a plane to take off or land.

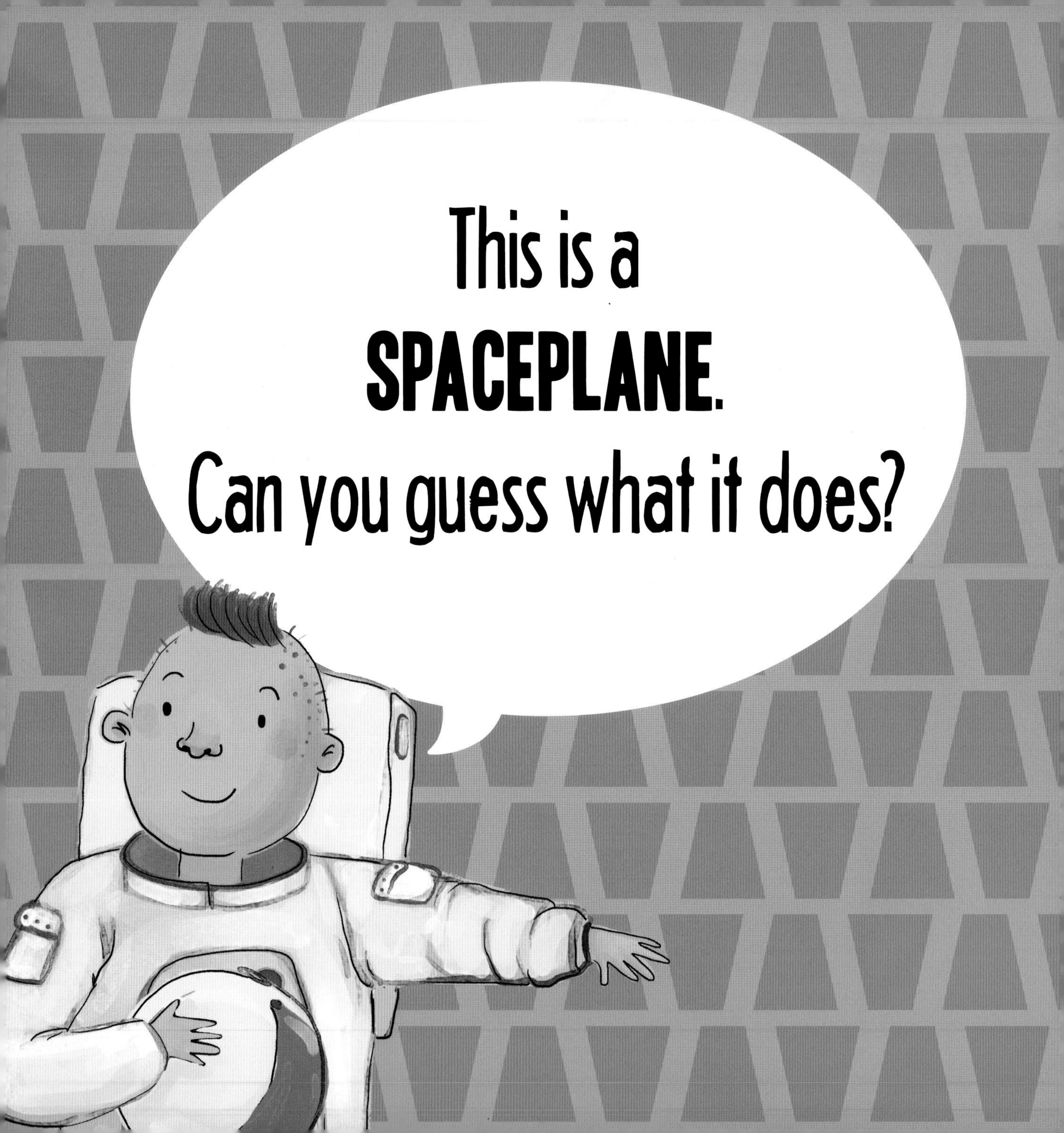
This is a
SPACEPLANE.
Can you guess what it does?

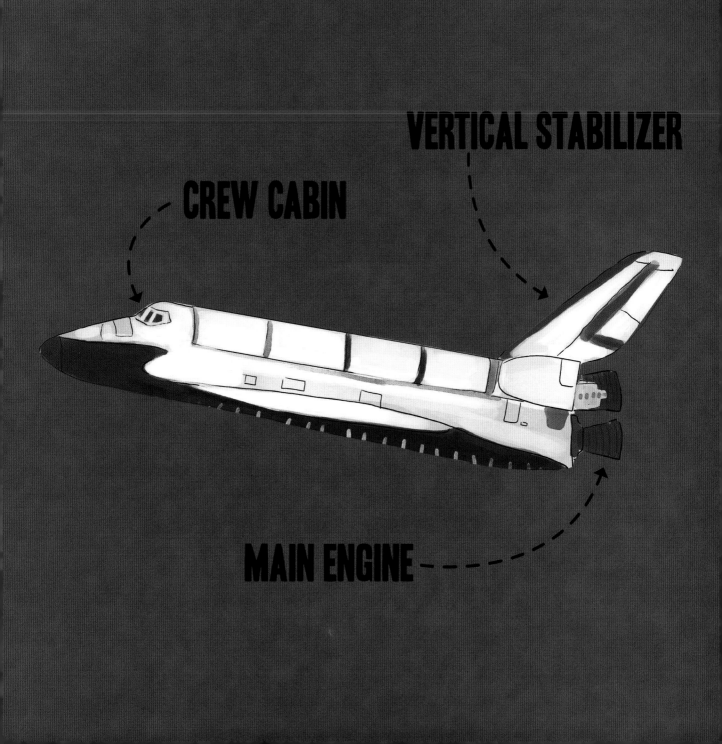

A spaceplane carries astronauts into space. It can be launched on a rocket and lands like an airplane.

We are the friendly fliers.

Can you guess all the places our crew can fly?

EVERYWHERE!

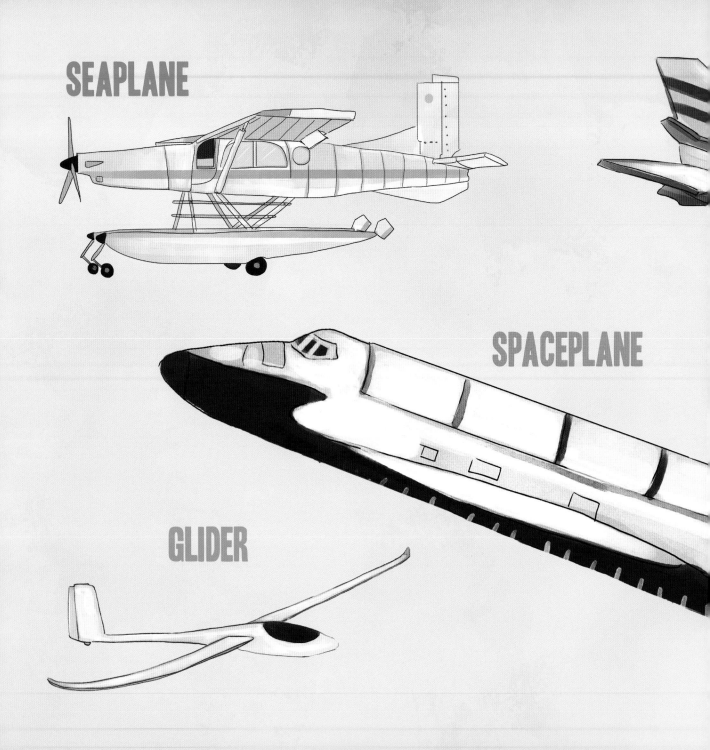

SEAPLANE

SPACEPLANE

GLIDER

JUMBO JET

HELICOPTER

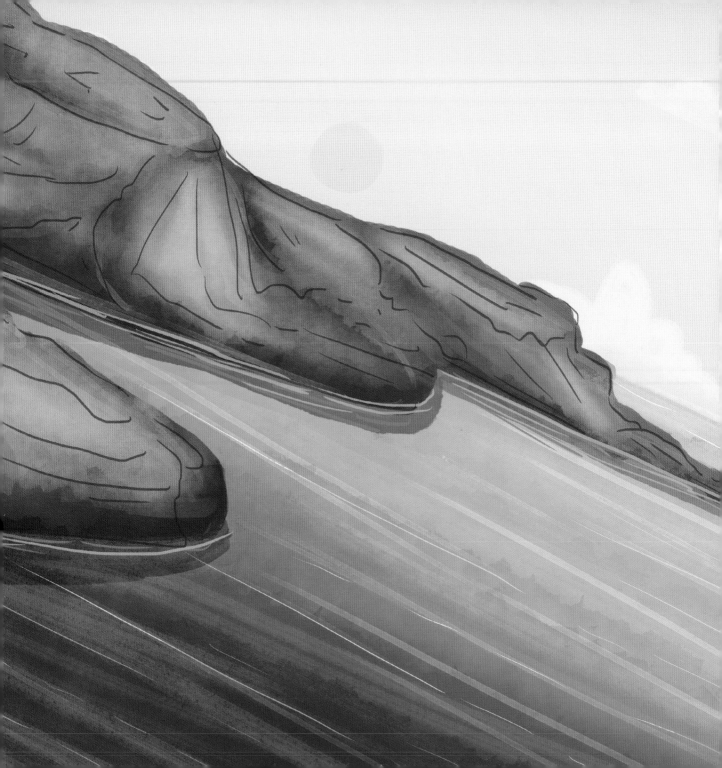